DRAMATIC HOURS
IN REVOLUTIONARY HISTORY

The
Story of Nathan Hale

BY

HENRY FISK CARLTON

Edited by CLAIRE T. ZYVE, Ph.D.
Fox Meadow School, Scarsdale, New York

HOW TO BE A GOOD RADIO ACTOR

The play in this book has actually been produced on the radio. Possibly you have listened to this one when you tuned in at home. The persons whose voices you heard as you listened, looked just as they did when they left their homes to go to the studio, although they were taking the parts of men and women who lived long ago and who wore costumes very different from the ones we wear today.

The persons whose voices you heard stood close together around the microphone, each one reading from a copy of the play in his hand. Since they could not be seen, they did not act parts as in other plays, but tried to make their voices show how they felt.

When you give these plays you will not need costumes and you will not need scenery, although you can easily arrange a broadcasting studio if you wish. You will not need to memorize your parts; in fact, it will not be like a real radio broadcast if you do so, and, furthermore, you will not want to, since you each have a copy of the book in your hands. All you will need to do is to remember that you are taking the part of a radio actor, that you are to read your speeches very distinctly, and that by your voice you will make your audience understand how you feel. In this way you will have the fun of living through some of the great moments of history.

HOW TO FOLLOW
DIRECTIONS IN THE PLAY

There are some directions in this play which may be new to you, but these are necessary, for you are now in a radio broadcasting studio, talking in front of a microphone. The word (*in*) means that the character is standing close to the microphone, while (*off*) indicates that he is farther away, so that his voice sounds faint. When the directions (*off, coming in*) are given, the person speaking is away from the microphone at first but gradually comes closer. The words (*mob*) or (*crowd noise*) you will understand mean the sound of many people talking in the distance.

Both the English and the dialect used help make the characters live, so the speeches have been written in the way in which these men and women would talk. This means that sometimes the character may use what seems to you unusual English. The punctuation helps, too, to make the speeches sound like real conversation; for example, you will find that a dash is often used to show that a character is talking very excitedly.

THE STORY OF NATHAN HALE

CAST

CAPTAIN NATHAN HALE
CAPTAIN WILLIAM HULL
GENERAL WASHINGTON
BOS'N
LIEUTENANT POND
SIMON CARTER
LIEUTENANT DREW [BRITISH]
MRS. CHICHESTER
CAPTAIN MONTRESSOR
PROVOST MARSHAL CUNNINGHAM

ANNOUNCER

We present here the story of the famous Revolutionary hero and martyr, Nathan Hale. For the first scene of our sketch, let us go to General Washington's headquarters in New York City. It is early September of the year 1776. In the Orderly room, outside of General Washington's private office, sits Captain William Hull, a member of the General's staff. Another officer comes through the door, Captain Hull glances toward the newcomer, jumps up, and exclaims—

HULL

Nathan Hale! As sure as I'm alive!

HALE

William Hull! Well, well, this is a surprise!

HULL

And you're a Captain! My congratulations, Nathan.

HALE

I might say the same to you, William!

HULL

What regiment are you in?

HALE

Knowlton's Rangers. And you?

HULL

Well, as you see, I'm on the General's staff. I envy you! Knowlton's Rangers, eh? Ah! There you have some chance for adventure! Some chance to distinguish yourself, while I—

HALE

Why, what's wrong with a staff appointment? I'd be honored if it were offered to me.

HULL

Yes, so was I. That's why I'm here. I was a lieutenant of artillery when General Washington asked me to join his staff. I jumped at the chance—

HALE

Who wouldn't?

HULL

I wouldn't, again! Why, all I've done for two months is write letters, sit at a desk, answer questions, and run errands! It's no duty for a man who craves action!

HALE

Yes, William, you have always been a fire eater.

HULL

Well, I eat no fire here, I can tell you. Now will you trade jobs with me?

HALE

If General Washington asks me to—I'll do it— though you haven't made it sound like a very attractive job, William.

HULL

Perhaps I've overdone it, Nathan—

HALE [laughing]

No use trying to crawl out of it now, William.

HULL

But you—you're more used to this sort of thing than I am. You're a schoolmaster—used to books and quills and letter writing.

HALE

That's true enough. You never had much love for books—as I remember it you were rather a trial to the dominie back home—by the way, what do you hear from South Coventry?

HULL

Not much—almost every man in the town enlisted.

HALE

Yes, I keep running across South Coventry men everywhere I go. It's a little town, but it has certainly done its duty well in this war.

HULL

If others had done as well, we wouldn't be in such dire straits now!

HALE

Things do look pretty black for us.

HULL

Black! They couldn't be blacker!

HALE

Have you any idea what the General's next move
will be?

HULL

No!—and what's more, I don't think he knows. It all
depends on General Howe's movements, and what
those will be nobody knows.

HALE

Is General Washington in his office now?

HULL

Yes. Did you come to see him?

HALE

I was ordered to report to him.

HULL

And here I've been keeping you out here—that
shows what a good staff officer I am! I'll announce
you at once. [*knock*]

WASHINGTON [*off*]

Yes, come in.

HULL

Sir, Captain Hale of Knowlton's Rangers awaits your pleasure.

WASHINGTON [*off*]

Ask him to come in at once, Captain.

HULL

Yes, sir. [*closer*] General Washington will see you now, Captain Hale.

HALE

Thank you.

HULL [*low*]

I'll wait out here for you. Come right in here! [*door closes*]

HALE

Captain Hale reports as ordered, sir.

WASHINGTON

Come in, Captain—come in!

HALE

Thank you, sir.

WASHINGTON

Will you sit here?

HALE

Thank you, sir.

WASHINGTON

Colonel Knowlton informs me that you and your company have been assigned to cover the North Shore line of Long Island Sound.

HALE

Yes, sir!

WASHINGTON

Well, Captain Hale, I am seriously in need of exact information which you may be able to secure.

HALE

What is that, sir?

WASHINGTON

Lord Howe's plans!

HALE

Yes, sir!

WASHINGTON

Can you get them?

HALE

I can try, sir.

WASHINGTON

You don't seem daunted by the magnitude of the undertaking.

HALE

It is an order, sir.

WASHINGTON

Well, my boy, no man knows better than I the impossibility of some orders.

HALE

But, sir—

WASHINGTON

I hope, though, that this is not impossible. I have to have the information. The safety of my whole army depends upon it. I must know particularly where General Howe intends to strike next.

HALE

Yes, sir.

WASHINGTON

If he comes across the East River, we can protect ourselves and keep out of his way. But if he comes across Long Island Sound—do you realize what that may mean to us?

HALE

Yes, sir. He can cut off our retreat.

WASHINGTON

Exactly! So that's what I must know.

HALE

I'll find out for you, sir.

WASHINGTON

Good! Now, Captain, you may go about your task in any way you see fit. I suggest two or three alternatives. First, you may tempt one of the enemy or a Tory who has access to the British lines, with a sum of money. You may draw on me for whatever is necessary.

HALE

Yes, sir.

WASHINGTON

Or you might make a sally across the Sound, capture a prisoner or two, and secure bits of information.

HALE

Yes, sir.

WASHINGTON

Or, though I hate to suggest it, you might go yourself in disguise to the British lines, but that should be only in a last desperate effort.

HALE

I understand, sir.

WASHINGTON

Or if you could get in touch with certain persons on Long Island who have been of service to us before—let's see—there is a shoemaker in Jamaica—what is his name—oh, here it is—Simon Carter.

HALE

Simon Carter. Yes, sir.

WASHINGTON

If you can find any way to get in touch with him—

HALE

I'll find a way, sir.

WASHINGTON

The password is "Liberty" used twice in your first sentence to him.

HALE

Yes, sir.

WASHINGTON

I don't know what he can do for you, but he is trustworthy and he may have some information.

HALE

I'll see him, sir.

WASHINGTON

Now, Captain, I don't want you to go yourself unless it is absolutely necessary. But I must have General Howe's plans as soon as possible.

HALE

Yes, sir. I understand. I'll see that you get them, sir.

WASHINGTON

Good! I believe you will, Captain. Good day.

HALE

Good day, sir. [*door closes*]

HULL [coming in]

Well, Nathan, what news?

HALE

I've got a job.

HULL

On the staff?

HALE

No. I'm afraid it's more hazardous than that.

HULL

You're lucky! A hazardous job! Say, what I wouldn't give to be in your shoes! What is it? Are you at liberty to tell?

HALE

Of course I'll tell you, William. I'm to discover General Howe's plan of action.

HULL [whistles]

I should say you had drawn a hazardous assignment! I'd call it a labor of Hercules!

HALE

Perhaps.

HULL

How are you going about it?

HALE

There's only one sure way of doing it.

HULL

Yes—and what's that?

HALE

I'll go myself into the enemy lines.

HULL

In disguise?

HALE

Of course.

HULL

That may involve serious consequences, Nathan.

HALE

I know it, but I think it's my duty.

HULL

Listen, Nathan. Let me go instead. It's more in my line.

HALE

No, William. The General has assigned me to the duty.

HULL

But he didn't order you to act the spy, did he?

HALE

No.

HULL

And he doesn't expect you to.

HALE

He expects me to get Howe's plans.

HULL

Look here—if I get permission to leave here, won't you let me go in your place?

HALE

I'm afraid not, William.

HULL

Listen to reason! You have a father and mother; you're engaged to be married. If by chance you were captured—well, I hate to think of it. But I'm alone in the world, it wouldn't make any difference what happened to me. Let me go!

HALE

It's no use, William. I appreciate your sentiment; but General Washington has given me a duty to perform, and I'd be a poor kind of soldier if I turned it over to anyone else simply because it involved danger.

HULL

Let me go with you, at least!

HALE

Well, if you can get permission, I'd be glad to have you go part of the way with me—though I must go into the enemy lines alone!

HULL

But—

HALE

I insist on that! There is added risk in two of us trying to work under disguise.

HULL

Oh, very well. Have it your way. When do we start?

HALE

Early tomorrow morning.

HULL

I'll get permission to accompany you at once.

ANNOUNCER

So early the next morning Hull and Hale started out together. They went into Connecticut and began looking for some means of crossing the Sound to the North Shore of Long Island. When they arrived near Norwalk they heard that an American gunboat was lying offshore. They determined to row out to it as soon as night came.

Our next scene is just after dark. Nathan Hale has put on his disguise, while William Hull has found a rowboat, and now draws up to the shore where Nathan is waiting for him.

HALE

Hello, William, that you?

HULL

It's me, right enough. Come on, climb in.

HALE

All right. Hold her there while I get aboard.

HULL

Easy, you'll have to jump for it! This is as close as I can come with this old tub.

HALE

Steady now! Here I come—all right! I didn't even get my feet wet!

HULL

Let me take a good look at your disguise. Hm— brown homespun suit—yes—that's a poor enough fit even for a penniless schoolmaster. And that hat! Yes, it'll disguise you all right.

HALE

I hope so. Give me an oar, I'll help you pull to the gunboat.

HULL

Here you are. [*rattle of oar in oarlock*] All ready?

HALE

Pull away, [*noise of regular rattle of oars in the lock and the swish of water continuing*]

HULL

Where are you going first, Nathan?

HALE

I don't know. I'll have to let circumstances direct me.

HULL

Are you going directly to that shoemaker the General referred you to?

HALE

No, not directly. I'll see what I can do without any help at first.

HULL

You better change your mind and let me go with you.

HALE

It's no use, William. I won't change my mind.

HULL

You always were stubborn, Nathan.

HALE

Perhaps. There's the gunboat, William!

HULL

Sure that's it?

HALE

No doubt of it.

HULL

Shall I hail them?

HALE

Let's pull in a little closer.

HULL

All right, pull away. There's no light aboard.

HALE

No—there wouldn't be. These waters are alive with British boats.

HULL

There! That's close enough! Give 'em a call now!

HALE

Ahoy, there!

BOS'N [*distance*]

Ahoy! Look sharp there! Don't come any closer! Who are you, and what do you want?

HALE

I want to speak to your Captain.

BOS'N

Who are you?

HALE

An officer of the Continental army!

BOS'N

Stand by—I'll report you.

HALE [*low*]

All right, William, as soon as I go aboard, row back to shore, and wait ten days for me. If I've not returned by then, go back and report me as lost.

HULL

Now, listen, Nathan! I've come this far with you, let me go—

HALE

We've settled all that, William, not once but several times.

HULL

Oh, all right.

POND [distance]

Ahoy, there! What's wanted?

HALE

I wish to come aboard, sir, with your permission.

POND

Hello, there, your voice sounds familiar. You don't by any chance happen to be Captain Hale?

HALE

Yes, indeed. I'm Captain Hale. But you have the advantage of me, sir—

POND

Come aboard, come aboard, Captain. Don't you remember Lieutenant Pond? I was in your regiment at the siege of Boston.

HALE

Of course, I do, Pond. I'm glad to hear your voice.

POND

Come aboard, Captain, I'll lower a ladder for you.

HALE

Thank you.

POND

Bos'n!

BOS'N

Aye, aye, sir!

POND

Lower the ladder for Captain Hale!

BOS'N

Aye, aye, sir! [*gives orders for lowering ladder*]

HALE [during the confusion]

Good-by, William. I'll try to be back in a week.

HULL

Good luck to you, Nathan.

HALE

If by any chance I fail to return, will you see that my uniform and other effects are sent to my family?

HULL

Of course I will, Nathan.

POND

Come aboard, Captain Hale!

POND [coming in]

Here you are, careful now! Give me your hand and watch yourself—there!

HALE

Thank you.

POND

What kind of an outfit do you call that you've got on! I'd never have known you if I hadn't heard your voice.

HALE

That's good, Pond!

POND

Good, why?

HALE

Because I'm bound for the enemy lines.

POND

What? Not on spy duty, I hope?

HALE

Exactly. Will you give me passage to Long Island, and land me in some secluded spot?

POND

Why—yes—if you wish it.

HALE

You can do it without endangering yourself or your boat?

POND

There'll be no difficulty about landing you. There is, however, a British man-of-war, the *Halifax*, in these waters. We have to watch out for her. But it's dark enough tonight to be perfectly safe.

HALE

Good! Can we go at once?

POND

Yes, sir. [*calling*] Bos'n!

BOS'N

Aye, aye, sir!

POND

Get the ship under way for Long Island! Bring her into that secluded cove near Huntington! You know the place.

BOS'N

Aye, aye, sir! [*calling*] All hands on deck! Man the windlass! Weigh anchor! [*etc.*] [*mob, setting sails, etc.*]

POND

Well, Captain Hale. This is new business for you, isn't it?

HALE

Yes, I've been transferred to Knowlton's Rangers. Our business is to get information. And I am under orders to secure some information that I can get in no other way.

POND

Hm. It's not a sweet business.

HALE

It's in my country's service! It seems that you, too, Lieutenant Pond, are in a new business. How long have you been in the navy?

POND

Two weeks.

HALE

I'm glad I found you here—I might have had some difficulty in convincing a stranger that I was really an officer in the Continental army.

POND

That's true enough. You look—well—more like a country schoolmaster than anything else.

HALE

That's what I hope to pass for.

POND

How long will you be on Long Island?

HALE

I shall try to be through my business in a week. I wonder if you would meet me at the same place you are going to leave me—say, a week from tonight?

POND

I'll send a small boat ashore for you, soon after dark a week from tonight.

HALE

Good! I'll be there—unless—

POND

Yes?

HALE

Unless I am unexpectedly detained.

POND

Oh, sir—we won't even think of that!

ANNOUNCER

Our next scene is several days later, at the little shop of the shoemaker, Simon Carter, in Jamaica. Simon is sitting on his stool, hammering away at a half-finished boot, when he hears a knock at his door. [*knock*]

SIMON

Come in, come in, the door ain't locked! Come on in!

HALE

Is this the shop of Simon Carter, the shoemaker?

SIMON

It is, no less!

HALE

Are you at liberty today—at liberty to do a little work for me?

SIMON

Close the door!

HALE

There. [*door closes*]

SIMON [*low*]

Now—sir—I'll do what I can fer ye—in the cause of liberty. What is it?

HALE [*low*]

Have you any information for the General?

SIMON

Aye—a plenty!

HALE

Can you give it to me?

SIMON

It's all written out—careful.

HALE

Good! Give it to me.

SIMON

Jest a minute. Don't them boots of yours need new soles?

HALE

Why, I don't know. I think they'll do.

SIMON

Never! Ye must have new soles!

HALE

Why?

SIMON

See here? This here sole?

HALE

Yes?

SIMON

Well, listen—come close—

HALE

Yes?

SIMON

The sole is split—the notes are inside it!

HALE

Good! That's an excellent idea!

SIMON

Slickest thing ye ever see. And it's my own idea!

HALE

I wonder if you could hide some notes I've gathered in the same way?

SIMON

O' course I could. I'll resole both boots. Give me yer notes.

HALE

Here they are. [*rattle of paper*]

SIMON

Pshaw, now—what kind o' writin' is this?

HALE

It's Latin. I thought if they were discovered on me—

SIMON

O' course—no soldier—that is, no redcoat could read that furrin writin'. Well, I'll put it where they'll never find it. Here—right in this sole. Now sit down there and pull yer boots off an' I'll fix 'em up fer ye.

HALE

Good! It's an excellent hiding place. Here you are.

SIMON

Yer a schoolmaster, I take it from the looks o' ye?

HALE

That's what I've been passing for.

SIMON

Now, where's that awl? Oh, here it is. And what name be ye usin' hereabouts?

HALE

Call me Master Nathan. [*knock*]

SIMON

Oh, someone at the door.

HALE

Had I better hide?

SIMON

No, no! 'tis better that ye sit right over there in the dark corner. Ye look innocent enough. Come in!

DREW [coming in]

Good morning, Simon.

SIMON

Good morrow to ye, Lieutenant Drew! I've got yer boots all finished fer ye.

DREW

Right! You're hard at work, I see.

SIMON

Always hard at work, Lieutenant. Here are yer boots. I'll wrap them up fer ye.

DREW [*low*]

Who's that gentleman over there?

SIMON [*low*]

A customer—I'm fixin' his boots.

DREW

Know him?

SIMON

Never set eyes on him before.

DREW

Unless I'm much mistaken, I've seen him before—
but I can't place him.

SIMON

Eh? Here's yer boots, Lieutenant. An' come around
again when ye have need of a good shoemaker.

DREW

Thank you. I'm going to speak to him. [*louder*]
Good morning, sir.

HALE

Good morning, sir.

DREW

Haven't we met somewhere?

HALE

I think you're mistaken, Mr.—

DREW

Drew—Drew—Lieutenant on His Majesty's
gunboat, the *Halifax*. Are you a stranger
hereabouts?

HALE

Yes, sir.

DREW

Do you live on the Island?

HALE

Why—ah—yes, sir.

DREW

Where?

HALE

Ah—er—near—Huntington.

DREW

Ah yes—well, no doubt I've seen you over there. I'm often at Huntington.

HALE

Yes, sir, no doubt.

DREW [jovially]

Perhaps you know that delightfully charming lady who keeps the tavern—Mrs. Chichester?

HALE

Slightly—only slightly.

DREW

Hm! You should know her—a delightful soul. Well, good day—good day, Simon.

SIMON

Good day, Lieutenant. [*door closes*]

HALE

Now, where have I met that man?

SIMON

Then ye *have* met him? He wasn't mistaken?

HALE

I've seen him somewhere—but I can't place him.

SIMON

Well—as long as he can't place you, yer safe, but git out o' this town as soon as ye can.

HALE

I will.

SIMON

Are ye from Huntington?

HALE

Never there in my life, except late at night when I landed on the Island.

SIMON

Well, I'll git the boots fixed for ye—then git out fast! No use runnin' any risks.

HALE

You're right, Simon. I shall take every care not to run into that man again.

ANNOUNCER

Our next scene is a few days later. It is evening.
Darkness is just falling. Mrs. Chichester, the keeper
of the Huntington Tavern, is bustling about her
kitchen, when Lieutenant Drew enters the back
door.

DREW

Good evening, Mrs. Chichester.

MRS. CHICHESTER

Good evenin' to ye, Lieutenant Drew. And what are
ye doin' comin' into my kitchen, I'd like to know?

DREW

Your tavern room's crowded, and I thought perhaps
you'd serve me here.

MRS. CHICHESTER

Indeed, I'll do nothing of the kind. There's room
enough in the tavern room.

DREW

But I'll have no chance to talk to you out there. And
I'd as soon not eat as be deprived of your company.

MRS. CHICHESTER

Go along with ye! Come on out here into the tavern room or ye'll not git a bite to eat.

DREW

Your word is law—I can only obey.

MRS. CHICHESTER

Through this door—here.

DREW

Oh, very well—wait—

MRS. CHICHESTER

Now what's the matter?

DREW

Close the door, Mrs. Chichester! Did you take particular notice of the man sitting alone in the corner?

MRS. CHICHESTER

The nice-lookin' young feller in the brown suit?

DREW

That's the one. Do you know him?

MRS. CHICHESTER

Never set eyes on him before.

DREW

Then he's not from Huntington.

MRS. CHICHESTER

He is not! I know every young blood hereabouts. An' he's not a native here, I kin warrant ye that.

DREW

I have it!

MRS. CHICHESTER

What—don't scare a body to death! What have ye got?

DREW

I know where I've seen him! He's a rebel.

MRS. CHICHESTER

A rebel! Indeed! In my tavern? I'll go throw him out!

DREW

No! No! We must make certain first. But I think he's an officer in the rebel army. Some months ago I was captured near Boston. I escaped later. But while I was a prisoner, I saw this fellow—unless I'm much mistaken. I saw him again the other day in Jamaica, at the shoemaker's; and now—look at him—here through the crack in the door!

MRS. CHICHESTER

He's lookin' fer somethin'—out the winder.

DREW

He's watching the shore of the cove!

MRS. CHICHESTER

Lookin' fer a boat to fetch him away, I'll warrant ye!

DREW

Exactly! Now, Mrs. Chichester, let's set a trap for him. Will you help me?

MRS. CHICHESTER

I will that! A rebel—and like as not a spy—in my tavern!

DREW

Go in to him, engage him in conversation, then look out the window and remark that you see a small boat landing.

MRS. CHICHESTER

Aye, I'll do it.

DREW

If he starts up, I'll know he's my man.

MRS. CHICHESTER

And then?

DREW

Tell him you're mistaken. The darkness deluded you.

MRS. CHICHESTER

Yes?

DREW

A small boat from my ship, the *Halifax*, is waiting for me round the point. I'll bring it around with my crew and we'll apprehend him.

MRS. CHICHESTER

Good. Wait here—I'll go in now. [*door opens, laughter and talk swell up*]

MRS. CHICHESTER

I hope, sir, ye found the roast beef to yer liking.

HALE

Yes, thank you, madam.

MRS. CHICHESTER

Can I help ye to anything else, sir?

HALE

I think not, thank you.

MRS. CHICHESTER

I'm sorry we have such poor fare, sir, but the times are hard, what with the comin' and goin' of the troops; and the rebels cleaned out the place when they were here.

HALE

I've fared very well, Madam.

MRS. CHICHESTER

Oh look—there in the cove! D'ye see a small boat comin' into shore? I wonder what it can be doin' here?

HALE

Oh, indeed! I'm afraid I'll have to go, Madam! Let me pay my reckoning.

MRS. CHICHESTER

There—I guess my eyes deceived me. It's not a boat at all.

HALE

Ah!

MRS. CHICHESTER

What was that you said? Your reckoning? But sir, you've had no sweetmeat. Come, sit down, I'll bring ye a bit o' pastry.

HALE

But—

MRS. CHICHESTER

I'll take it much amiss if ye refuse me.

HALE

Thank you, Madam—I'll wait—bring your sweetmeat.

ANNOUNCER

As soon as Hale finished his meal at the tavern, he went to the shore of the cove to await the boat that he expected. After some time he heard the splash of oars. So sure was he that this was his boat that he stood up and called.

HALE

Hello, Pond, here I am! Right here!

DREW

Stand fast, put your hands up!

HALE

What—what's the meaning of this? Sir, I am a peaceable schoolmaster, you have no cause to apprehend me!

DREW

We'll soon see. Strike a light! Search him!

VOICE

Aye, aye, sir—here's your light.

DREW

Well, sir, I thought I'd seen you before. Now I know I have! I've placed you at last! You are an officer in the rebel army!

HALE

I tell you, sir, I am a poor schoolmaster!

DREW

We'll soon see. Find anything in his pockets?

VOICE

Not a thing, sir.

DREW

Rip his jacket to pieces, look in the lining and the seams!

VOICE

Yes, sir. [*sound of tearing cloth*]

HALE

Why am I suffering this indignity?

DREW

Anything there?

VOICE

Not a thing, sir.

DREW

Strip him—tear every piece of clothing to pieces!

VOICE

Aye, aye, sir.

HALE

I trust this is giving you some pleasure.

DREW

We're enjoying ourselves, aren't we, boys?

ALL

Aye, aye, sir.

VOICE

Here, sir—a piece o' paper.

DREW

Let's see it—ha—receipt for lodgings. Is that the best you can do?

VOICE

That's all there is, sir.

HALE

Perhaps, sir, now that you have ruined my clothes, you'll let me go.

DREW

I will not! I'll find where you've hidden your notes if I have to rip your skin off!

HALE

I am helpless, sir. But you must be satisfied that I have nothing on me. Can't you conclude your sport and let me go?

DREW

Look here, men—what about his boots?

VOICE

Nothing in them, sir.

DREW

He was having them resoled the other day! Ho, I'll wager that's where they are! Give me your knife, Bos'n!

VOICE

Here you are, sir.

DREW

Hm! There—ah, ha! I thought so! Papers— papers—I thought as much—bring the light nearer! Hm—what's this? Some foreign tongue—Ah! Latin. Who would have expected a rebel to know Latin?

HALE

I am a schoolmaster, sir.

DREW

Aye, and a spy as well—as these notes prove.

HALE

Can you read them?

DREW

My Latin is a little rusty, but I can make out the tenor of them. Hm—disposition of troops—

probable movements of army—yes, that will do! What have you to say to that, my fine rebel?

HALE

Nothing.

DREW

You don't need to. We've evidence enough to hang you as it is. Bring him along, men! [*mob noise*]

ANNOUNCER

So Hale was taken aboard the *Halifax* and delivered late the same night to General Howe, who, without the formality of a trial, turned him over to the Provost Marshal, William Cunningham, for execution the next day.

Our next scene is in the apple orchard of the Beekman estate on Manhattan. Hale has been marched out for his execution. He is standing under guard, near the tent of Captain John Montressor, who, as our scene opens, comes out of his tent, sees Hale, and speaks to him.

MONTRESSOR

Sir, I regret to see such a fine appearing young man in this situation.

HALE

You are kind to say so, sir.

MONTRESSOR

May I ask your name and rank?

HALE

I am Captain Nathan Hale, of the Colonial army.

MONTRESSOR

May I introduce myself? I am Captain John Montressor. Can I be of any assistance to you?

HALE

I should be deeply grateful, sir, if I could write a few lines to friends and relatives before I meet my fate.

MONTRESSOR

Will you come into my tent?

HALE

If my guard—

MONTRESSOR

I'll tend to the guard.

HALE

Thank you.

MONTRESSOR

You'll find quills, ink, and paper on my field desk.

HALE [*going*]

Thank you, sir.

VOICE

I say, halt there—where are you going?

MONTRESSOR

Never mind, Corporal! I'll be responsible for the prisoner.

VOICE

Very good, Captain, but the Provost Marshal won't like it! I can tell you that.

MONTRESSOR

I'll take all the blame. The Provost Marshal never likes anything, so that's no matter. Here, put this crown in your pocket.

VOICE

Right enough, sir. Thank you.

MONTRESSOR

Do you know anything about the prisoner?

VOICE

No, sir. Ah, sir! Here comes the Provost Marshal!

MONTRESSOR

Let me talk to him.

CUNNINGHAM [*coming up*]

Where's the prisoner? Guard! Where's the prisoner?

MONTRESSOR

Just at this moment, sir, he is writing a few notes in my tent.

CUNNINGHAM

Bring him out here!

MONTRESSOR

I'll get him, sir, if I may be allowed.

CUNNINGHAM

Go ahead, get him.

MONTRESSOR [*off*]

I'm sorry, Captain Hale, but the Marshal is waiting for you—have you finished your letters?

HALE [*off*]

Not quite, sir.

MONTRESSOR [*calling*]

He hasn't finished his letters, sir.

CUNNINGHAM

Fetch him along—he's written enough.

MONTRESSOR

I'm sorry, Captain.

HALE

Of course I'll come. May I ask you to deliver these letters at your first opportunity?

MONTRESSOR

Surely.

CUNNINGHAM

Guard, fall in around the prisoner.

VOICE

Guard, fall in—'ten—*shun*! Quick step—march! [*marching*]

CUNNINGHAM

Halt under the tree!

VOICE

Guard, halt!

CUNNINGHAM

Put the prisoner on the ladder!

HALE

It isn't necessary, sir—I can climb the ladder.

CUNNINGHAM

All right then, get up there. Put the halter around his neck, and blindfold him.

HALE

I can do that, too, sir.

CUNNINGHAM

All right, then, do it! And if you have any further statement or confession to make, now is the time to do it.

HALE

I only regret that I have but one life to lose for my country.

CUNNINGHAM

Humph! Now, guard, when I give the word, kick the ladder and let the rebel swing. Are you ready?

VOICE

Ready.

CUNNINGHAM

Steady—now! [*noise of ladder, gasp, etc.*] [*pause*] So let all spies, rebels, and traitors swing! March the guard off!

VOICE

Guard—fall in! Quick step—[*etc.*]

MONTRESSOR [*to himself*]

Poor fellow—and he's hardly more than a boy.

CUNNINGHAM

And now, Captain Montressor, I'll trouble you for those letters.

MONTRESSOR

Here they are, Marshal.

CUNNINGHAM

Ah—[*sound of tearing paper*]

MONTRESSOR

What are you doing, sir? Stop it! Don't tear those letters up!

CUNNINGHAM

I've already done it, Captain.

MONTRESSOR

What did you do that for? They were intrusted to me for delivery.

CUNNINGHAM

Well—they won't be delivered! The rebels shall never know they had a man who could die with such firmness!

ANNOUNCER

The next day, however, Captain Montressor carried the news to the American lines under a white flag and repeated to Hale's companions those words— which have come down to us: "I only regret that I have but one life to lose for my country!"

www.ingramcontent.com/pod-product-compliance
Lightning Source LLC
Chambersburg PA
CBHW032029040426
42448CB00006B/779